BLOOMIN'

Where Poetry and Growth Meet

Morgan Casteel

Fulton Books
Meadville, PA

Illustrated by Lindsey Shaw

Published by Fulton Books 2025

ISBN 979-8-89427-689-2 (paperback)
ISBN 979-8-89427-690-8 (digital)

Printed in the United States of America

Contents

Grow

Flourish

Heal

Grieving, the Process

every now and then
    the memories flood back
and i drown in the sea of mourning

The Hardest Part

all the little things remind me of you
your warmth radiating from the sun
your giggle in the sound of the creek flowing over
    the rocks
your favorite ice cream flavor dripping off the cone
but they still don't bring you back

Since You've Been Gone

every day i walk into a house
but it doesn't feel like home
    not since you left

What They Don't Tell You

home is not
> four walls and the roof over your head

home is where you are

loved
> welcomed
> and accepted

Trying to Cheer Me Up

i go to parties
    and bars
    and concerts
but even in all the crowds and happy faces
i can't help but feel
    so alone

The Hope

they say that
happiness and sadness—
they come in waves
if that's the case
      maybe one day i'll drown

Wishing Well

even in all my sadness
and grief
i continue to put on a brave face for my family—
i will be their wishing well
and i will give
and give
and give
until i am dry

To Be or Not to Be

i feel like an escaped criminal
walking on eggshells
    in my own house
my bedroom is my jail cell
    and my sanctuary all in one
where i can't hear the yelling or screaming

U-Turn

my whole life i have felt like
i keep going the wrong way
on a one-way street
and my body can't make a U-turn

Multiple Definitions

i am so afraid of love
afraid to fall
afraid to stay
afraid to get hurt
but i am also so deprived of it
    the affection
    the touch
    the warmth
sometimes i think that just maybe
    they're the same

Stepping Stone

every one step forward i take
the world pushes me back three
it's a never ending
vicious
cycle

Learn

Confusion

our love:
it was so open
      so honest
      so wholesome
      and special
until it wasn't

Even the Stars Fall

every time you feel
    lost
    or exhausted
take a step back
and look at how far you've come
remind yourself of all the
    mountains
    you have
    climbed
to get to where you are

Who You Are

you are all the things
i wanted love to be
and all the things
i never even dreamed it could be

Things That Fall

1. leaves
2. rain
3. stars
4. snowflakes
5. trees
6. babies
7. tears

but the best of them all
is when i fell for you

There is Evil in Comparison

you are all the beautiful things in this life
like the sky
      when the orange sun breaks through the clouds
      during the last few minutes of the sunset
like the tall wheat grass
      when the gentle wind is blowing on a fall morning

The Smallest Things

you deserve all the beautiful things in this life
    love notes on your dash
    a vase full of flowers on the table
    honesty & loyalty
you deserve to be reminded every day
    just how loved and cherished you are

In Color

it's funny to me
just how different we all see the world
every set of eyes sees a different hue
but when you meet the right one
　　　and the colors blend together
it's the most beautiful thing

I Can't Get Enough

i used to cringe when a boy
would call me "babe" or "baby"
but when you say it
        before a sentence
        or after you compliment me
i can't get enough

I'm Fine

sometimes i get caught off guard
when someone asks me if
    i'm okay
it's been a while since i heard that
and sometimes i can't find the words
"i'm fine" comes out of my mouth
before i even have time to think
    i'm not fine
    can't you see?

Grow

The Roaring River

oh, but darling
you are a river
    strong and mighty
rocks try to break you
mountains and valleys bend and twist you
but you keep on flowing

Grieving, the Outcome

i hope you're looking down
and smiling
at all the progress i've made
    it's all for you

People Are Puzzles Too

in all my years
of dealing with brokenness
        i have found
it is easier to leave people
        better than we found them
so the next person doesn't have to
        rearrange the pieces

The Truth

i was afraid, you knew that
i wasn't trying
honestly, i may have even been pushing away
but we fell in love
    so deeply
it didn't feel like falling

Snake in the Grass

my mom used to tell me
  watch out for the snake in the grass
i grew up where the trees are taller than all the buildings
with five stoplights in my hometown
i was used to snakes
  copperheads
  black racers
  cottonmouths
but that's not what she was talking about
and i learned that the hard way

Peace

i find peace in knowing
that even when the stars fall
and the rain pours
and the night is cold and dark
    the sun will rise again

What You Find

in your hardest
    and darkest
moments
you will find
    peace
in knowing
    God's got you
    tomorrow is a new day

Religion

i grew up southern baptist
    church every sunday
    don't forget sunday school
i have always been religious
    but i have also questioned
    i'm curious
all religions are so different
yet the same
all of them have one common theme
    love others
why is that so hard?

The Day

i remember the day i lost my mother
one month before my eighth birthday
i remember the people looking down
     feeling sorry for me
that day changed me
that day gave me a reason to live
and while i'd do anything to change it,
i am forever thankful for the person i've become

Curious

as i get older
the more i long for the unknown
i want a life
filled with passion and joy
but what does that look like?
to me, it looks like
loving you

Take Notice

we live in a world
where you can do anything
be anything
get anything
but take notice
not everything is
    good for you

This One's for You

my mother spent every free moment reading
she loved books
        and the way they made her feel emotions.
i know she's looking down now, smiling with tears
        in her eyes
because she knows
this one's for her

Take Your Time

it is okay to slow down
    take a break
    take a breath
it takes bees many long days
    and hard work
to make one teaspoon of honey
and that's one of the sweetest things on earth

Flourish

Home

i have finally found my home
but it has nothing to do with where i lay my head
i have found my home in wherever you are

Be Gentle with Yourself

my daily reminders:
    no one cares about the pimple on my chin
    the scratch on my leg from my excited puppy
    the hair that fell out of my clip
they just love me

Those Three Words

i love you
that statement was weird for me to say
but now
i can hardly go a few hours without saying it

To Describe You

i was once asked what you were like
and i couldn't find the words to describe that
you are
the way the sun dances on the water
you make me feel like the sunset
     after a long day of rain

When You Know

the best feeling in the world
is realizing that i loved something
just by watching you love it

The Love They Wish They Had

growing up i was told i deserved the
    "i never knew how good it could be"
kind of love
well, my friend,
    i found it

Even at 3:00 a.m.

i find peace in knowing
that at 2:00 p.m.
when i haven't had any water yet
or 9:00 p.m.
when i fall asleep during a movie
or even at 3:00 a.m.
when i'm rolled up in all the blankets that i stole from
    you
    you still love me
    and always will

Growth

as a child i wondered
how could the flowers sprout through the asphalt
in all its hardness
but the sprouts taught me the art of growth
and the petals taught me the art of letting go after
    tough battle

Cheers

here's to you, my friend
for being gentle with yourself
and for fresh grace
    every day

Never Forgotten

out of all this mess
there is one thing i learned-
i am not living my life without you
i am living my life for you
and spreading the love you left behind

Out of Darkness Comes Light

there are many evil things in this world
but what made her beautiful
was the courage she had
        to continue to shine
despite all the bad that tried to consume her

The Pot Calling the Kettle

i need to remind myself
that even i need to take the advice
that i so freely give to others.

Time to Flourish

because in the end, sweet girl,
you will realize that all the hard things you had to endure
forced you to become the best you

The Importance of You

prioritize you
and your growth
this world is full of people
    and things
that will try to shove you down
but let that only
    make you stronger

What I Believe In

i have found my crutch
    and my hope
in Jesus
after all my faults & flaws
    my sin and shame
He does not shun me
He smiles with open arms
and says
    welcome home
what more could you ask for?

Flourishing

we want our crops to grow
  tall and strong
  to flourish
so we can feed our family generously
but why do we never encourage ourselves to flourish?

How I Live My Life

there is nothing i want more
in this life
than joy.
i get to choose the
      people that uplift me
      things that make me smile
      hobbies that warm my heart
and i get to be
      unapologetically me.
i hope you do too.

About the Author

Growing up in the small town of Powhatan, Virginia, Morgan learned the value of hard work from a young age. She wrote her first book while working six days a week and taking a full course load from Liberty University. Morgan experienced the loss of her mother at a very young age but realized then how much a person can mean to someone else and how much someone can grow with the help from the right green thumb. She combined her love of plants with her love of poetry in hopes that this book is what we all need to flourish.